DARK THOUGHTS ON COLD NIGHTS

COLBY BETTLEY

Copyright

COPYRIGHT ©2024

Dark Thoughts On Cold Nights | Colby Bettley | All rights reserved.

No part of this book may be reproduced in any written, electronic, recording, or photocopying without written permission of the publisher or author. The exception would be in the case of brief quotations embodied in the critical articles or reviews and pages where permission is specifically granted by the publisher or author.

This is a work of fiction. Names, characters, businesses, places, events and incidents are either the products of the author's imagination or used in a fictitious manner. Any resemblance to actual persons, living or dead, or actual events is purely coincidental.

First Edition | Publication Date: January 14, 2024

Cover design by V. Domino @3crows.author.services

Editing by Novel & Noted by Colby Bettley @colby_bettley

Formatting by V. Domino @3crows.author.services

dark thoughts

cold nights

Dedication

To the people who feel like they're alone in the dark...

dark thoughts

cold nights

Author Note

This collection of poems is designed to make you feel less alone in the world when things seem bleak. It can be hard to evaluate how we feel or the darkness of our thoughts, which results in us burying the feelings a lot of the time. But it's important that we give ourselves credit for fighting for survival every day. No matter how dark the world seems, how isolated you feel, please know that you're not alone.

And if you ever need someone to talk to, please reach out. My DMs and emails will always be open for anyone who needs it.

I

Unwanted

They said

I was wanted.

Big smiles

And promises of love.

But

At some point

They stopped wanting me.

2

Undone

I am undone

by your smile

by your heart

by the way you love me.

I am undone

by your touch

by your secrets

by the way you own me.

I am undone

because you pulled me apart

a frayed edge

a loose thread.

I am undone.

3

DROWNING

DROWNING
in your love.
In life.
In loneliness.
I feel it seeping
into my throat,
burning my insides,
washing me away.
Drowning
in my own head.
In sadness.
In lies I can't unravel.
I feel it

beckoning me,
pulling me to the edge
until I am nothing.
Drowned.

4

I could love you,
But then I'd lose myself.

5

THE SCARS HAVE LONG SINCE FADED

but i can still see them

see the lines where

i pressed my blade

against my skin

hoping that my sadness

would bleed out

sometimes i look at them

the scars that aren't scars anymore

and i ache to do it again

because i did bleed once

but my sadness is still here

                                        haunting me every day

6

WHISPERS

can still be heard

even from behind

closed doors

7

It feels wrong

to be this sad when I have you.

You make me smile

and laugh

and cry

in the best possible way.

But sometimes

on my loneliest nights

you don't see me

or my breaking heart.

I'm laying in bed

my eyes wet with tears

and all I want is for you to see me.

8

I think omissions

are almost like lies

because when you keep things from me

my heart breaks the same way

9

Y‌ou expect me to be better

and almost perfect

but you won't try for me.

> Why won't you try?

10

I never expected
to feel so lonely
when I love you so hard it hurts.

II

You asked me once to tell you if I was ever angry or sad at you. But how can I tell you and watch as my sadness becomes yours? So even when I'm sad or angry or broken inside, I'll cry myself to sleep instead of telling you. Because hurting myself more will always be more preferable than seeing you suffer.

12

I miss creating art

and having paint across my skin.

The feeling of calm

when my brushes glide on canvas.

But I can't paint anymore

because art is about expression

soulfulness

beauty

and I feel empty inside.

I cannot create

when I feel nothing for the world.

13

It has become so easy

to wear a mask

that I no longer know the true image
of my self.

14

I don't think I'm a whole person.

Not on my own,

Because when you are silent

Or someone leaves

I become an empty shell

Of being.

It is like all of the life in me

Suddenly evaporates

And I become a ghost of a person.

A fraction of a human.

I am the remnants of who I am

When you are around.

                                        Please don't leave.

15

IN LOVING MEMORY

OF ME.

16

I don't know when my life turned into this cosmic mess.

A beautiful creation of particles

which now drift aimlessly through time.

I am alive and living

but it feels as though I am not.

Chaos is second nature in my mind

though I fear that part of myself.

Normalcy is the wish of many

and it is human nature to strive for it.

The harder I wish for even a fraction of ordinary days

in an ordinary life

makes me far more chaotic than anticipated.

Perhaps I am destined to remain

a firework of confusion amid

the prophetic beauty of life.

17

I would let the weight of the world crush me

if it meant

you never had to feel it touch you

18

Hatter Isn't Mad

What if the Hatter wasn't really mad?
Perhaps Hatter was a visionary,
Saw the world in a way that was deemed abnormal.
Hatter could create masterpieces at his fingertips,
Bring beauty and uniqueness to life in minutes.
He was praised for his creations,
So long as they were what the people wanted.
When Hatter wanted to make things for himself,
And the people he loved and cared about,
His masterful skill was mocked.
For Hatter was a genius,
But ingenuity is often called instability
If it is perceived by the wrong lens.

What if Hatter wasn't really mad?

Hatter just saw the world differently from everyone else.

19

I spend all day

Every day

Wearing a mask

Smiling

Laughing

Being the person

Everyone wants me to be

At night

Every night

The mask slips away

My tears fall

Slowly at first

Then become wracking sobs

Until I am nothing

But the empty

Cold

Darkness which lives inside of me.

20

Don't leave me / Please / I know your demons are pulling you under / But I'm stronger than them / I will be your anchor to this world / And promise to help you push through / So please don't leave me / Because I can't bear the thought / Of a world without you in it / Or a life lived without you / By my side

21

Loneliness creeps in

Threatening to consume me.

On those days

The only thing that saves me

Is you.

22

A NEVER-ENDING CYCLE

of dark thoughts

plaguing me

drowning me

threatening to wreck me

23

You're not mine

but I'll protect you at all costs

as though you are.

When you cry

I feel that pain.

But when you smile

it feels brighter than the sun.

You're not mine by blood

but I'd choose you every lifetime over.

You may not be mine

but I love you like you are.

24

I don't tell anyone that I'm not okay

because when they see me sad

and can't do anything to help

it breaks my heart more.

I see them in pain

because of *my* pain

and so I'd rather keep it bottled up

than see them uncomfortable and sad too.

25

The pain of losing you

Is too much to bear

Every night

I cry tears of grief

Because you left a hole in my heart

When you left

I don't need final words

Or a perfect goodbye

I just need to know

I'll see you on other side

So that this heartache

Will be worth it

26

HEALING ISN'T LINEAR

And it feels like a damn maze.

27

No matter where you are
Or what you're doing,
I'll love you anyway.

28

It's cold and icy outside,
The sky dark and moody.
On nights like these,
I think a lot.
Of past experiences,
Love lost,
Friendships gone awry.
I blanket myself against the cold,
With the pain of years gone by.

29

I hate that I love you so much

Because I love you more

Than I love myself.

So even when you hurt me

I close my eyes

And cry instead.

I'll never tell you

So that you never hurt

The way that I do.

30

I REWATCH OLD SHOWS / REPEAT REPEAT REPEAT / EVERYTHING ON A loop / watching for the episodes i know will make me cry / so that i can feel anything / something / the release i'm searching for

31

Why am I never enough?
No matter how hard I try
Or how much I love
It's never enough.
I am always second.
Second best
Never quite good enough
To be loved the most.
It's a selfish thought
But just once
I wish someone would pick me first

32

Odd One Out

I've never been good

At fitting in

At being part of the crowd

One of the inner circle

So I can't escape this thought

That you won't choose me

Because I'm not like them

And I don't have the capacity to pretend I am

I know that you'll figure out

That I don't belong

And you'll wish I was gone

Which will break my heart

So I'm trying to fake it

But all I hear is
My mind telling me
I'm the odd one out

33

People always ask

If a tree falls in the forest

But nobody is around to hear it

Does it make a sound?

> Similarly, I wonder to myself
> If I keep everything bottled up
> And nobody pays attention
> Will anyone hear my heart break?

34

If soulmates exist,
I believe Death is mine.

35

Little witch says a spell

Hoping magic can save her

36

If I could wish for anything

It would be for more time with you.

Oh, how I miss you.

37

There's nobody else

I would ever stick around for.

38

To be honest, you are my worst nightmare

Because I love you so much

That the thought of losing you

Haunts my every thought

39

The mark of a tiger

A TIGER HAS STRIPES

And people see it as a warrior

So why is it that

When people see my stripes

They view me as a coward?

My stripes show me I survived

And you can never take that from me

40

One day I will learn

that it isn't selfish

to prioritise myself

41

Can you imagine what it's like

to feel so sad

and empty

that nothing matters anymore?

42

YOU ARE THE PUREST SOUL

AND I FEAR TO KNOW YOU

TO LOVE YOU

WILL ONLY CORRUPT YOU

43

Would anyone really care

if I disappeared?

44

There is such a thing as

platonic soulmates.

A love so pure

nobody else can really comprehend.

When I say

I'm in love with them

I mean it with my entire soul.

Because if I had to choose anyone,

I would choose them.

Romantic love can fade

or leave

but I know my love for them won't.

45

Cold metal

On soft skin

Tiger marks long since healed

Yet they still feel

Like gaping wounds

46

I want someone / to be there for me / the way I am / for everyone else. / Someone to deal with / the sadness I feel / to tell they'll be by my side / no matter what moods / I go through. / If I'm angry / they'll calm the storm. / If I'm sad / they'll be my anchor to the living. / They will tell me / how much I matter to them / and that I can never be replaced. / Because while I cling on / for dear life / I can feel myself / slipping through the cracks.

47

Nothing feels lonelier

Than being sad

And nobody seeing it

48

Sometimes I need you to push me

to tell you how I feel

because I'll never tell you first time

in case it makes you sad

but keeping it bottled up

threatens to break me entirely

49

isn't it amazing

how

that one smile

can light up your entire life?

But isn't it sad
that
the loss of it
can plunge you further
into the abyss?

50

I wasn't born

Wanting to die

51

How am I supposed to move on

from losing you?

I didn't get a chance

to tell you how much I love you.

You left me behind

and now all I know

is the pain of grieving you.

FRAGILE

Love is a beautiful and
fragile thing

Perhaps that is why
I'm so scared of it

Because I know
the weight of my pain
would shatter it

53

I need you to tell me

That you'd choose me

So that I know

I'm enough for someone

54

We are born
to be special
an integral part
of the world's revolution

And yet
my mind often thinks
that our most important role
is to become one with the earth
after our final breath

55

—I'M SORRY YOU HAD TO SUFFER
MEETING ME

56

SILENCE

A myriad of thoughts crushing me

But no words

No voice

Just silence

57

Sections of the Day

What's wrong?
What's wrong is that
For ¾ of the day
I cry and wish i was dead
And for that other ¼
I sleep and imagine
My wish came true

58

I'm scared that my darkness

will infect you

and you'll hate me

for pulling you under

with me

59

Losing you ruined my life

And the lives of everyone I love

But I can't even be angry

Because it wasn't your choice

Each day that anger

Turns inward

Since that's easier

Than processing saying

Goodbye.

60

IF I JUST STOPPED TALKING

Would anyone notice?

If I just stopped existing

Would anyone miss me?

"I would." she said

61

My mind is a thunderstorm

And there is nothing I can do

To stop it destroying the garden

Of my life

62

If only love could save me

I'd never have to worry about dying

63

I'm sorry I'm so sad

all the time

I promise

I'm trying to be better

64

FEAR

I'VE NEVER BEEN SO SCARED
to lose a person
as I am
of losing
you

65

I'm tired of keeping a smile on my face
pretending I'm happy
and that everything's fine
when inside I feel like I'm screaming
just hoping someone will finally hear

66

Silence doesn't feel so empty
When I have you

67

If I listen carefully

Sometimes I hear your voice

Carried by the sea

In waves gone by

68

I'm not ungrateful for the life I've been given.
It's just that if there was a choice, I'd give my life up for someone more deserving.

69

Little Pills

Little pills, little pills
Ones that are meant to help
When your mood starts to dip
Take your little pills

I don't want to take them
And I think they make me worse
But what else can I do
When just living feels like a curse

Take your little pills
And pretend it's all okay
Ignore the way they make you feel
Cause they might work for you someday

. . .

Two weeks of side effects
But hey, don't worry
The little pulls will fix you
And life will be just sunny

I hate these stupid little pills
And I hate myself too
Though the thought of life before
Makes me power through

Ones that make you cry
Ones that make you numb
Little pills can't fix it all
But at least they'll stop me wanting to die

70

I'M SO HAPPY YOU EXIST

Even if I'm sad that I do

71

Tears stop

Laughter fades

All that's left is the memories

Of me and you

72

IF EYES ARE THE WINDOWS TO THE SOUL / THEN I HAVE SEEN EVERY
inch / of what makes you / the magic person / i love so much /
because i can't stop / staring at you

73

I'll never be as good a person
as I'm trying to be
but believe me when I say
I'll never give up

74

Love Through It All

You say you'll love me through it all but how can that be when I don't love myself?

How can you love the version of me too weak to shower or smile or process anything when I'm in a depressive episode?

How can you love the person I am when all I see is the darkness of the world?

There are times when my mind becomes nothing but anxiety and my fingers bleed as a result.

You won't love me when I can't breathe because the world is too loud for me or when just opening my eyes makes me want to cry.

You say you'll love me through it all, but I can't even love myself at the best of times.

How could I expect you to?

75

Overthinking means my brain doesn't stop.

I have a thousand scenarios playing out like a horrifying blooper reel.

Pilot episodes of my nightmares, testing to see what makes me snap.

76

I want to know everything about you
All your little stories
The things that have hurt you
And the love you've shown

If there was a way that I could live forever
Just so that I could hear you talk
I'd make the bargain in a heartbeat

I want to know your pain
Understand your heart
And stand by your side
Because then I'll understand
I'll know.

77

Understanding myself more

Feels like a really messed up way

Of knowing my brain doesn't work the way it should.

78

For all my mistakes,
knowing you will never be one.

79

Why am I kind

to everyone

but myself?

80

You, my love, are like January. A fresh start. A celebration of the future. A way to rewrite history. You, my love, are the goodness we've all been waiting for.

81

Little Me

Oh, little me

I'm sorry for what I've done

You had so much hope for life

A bright future planned

And I have turned into the monster

Stopping it from coming to fruition

82

I TRIED TO FIX MYSELF

BUT I MADE IT WORSE INSTEAD.

IS THERE STILL HOPE?

PLEASE, TELL ME THERE IS.

83

i cherish those first few minutes of waking
when the world is still a blur
because i can forget the things that plague me
and pretend like i'm at peace

84

Look into my eyes

And you'll see

The ghosts of my past

85

I crave solitude

And yet

Loneliness is suffocating me

86

I'll miss you forever

Even if I'm smiling

Or outwardly happy

The hurt of losing you

Will always be inside

87

I THINK TO MUCH

And I don't really know how to stop it.

I think and I think and I think

Until my mind is an anxious tangle of words and worries.

I don't feel normal

Or sane

Or even human.

I feel like a ghost

Watching the rest of the world live

While I try my best to mimic what they do.

And just once

I want to stop thinking

Long enough to feel something instead.

88

If God told me to pick a star from the sky,
and I could keep it forever,
I'd decline politely.
Instead, I'd ask
if I could just keep you.

89

ONE DAY

I will be someone's first choice.

OR MAYBE ONE DAY

I will choose myself.

90

Dear self,

Loving you is not a hardship or the burden you think it is. Allow yourself to love the broken parts of you and maybe you'll see just how beautiful you are.

Sincerely,
Me

About the Author

Colby Bettley is a bestselling author and poet from Scotland, so if you aren't reading this in an accent, you're doing it wrong. She splits her time between her editing company (Novel and Noted), writing, and also writing but under a different name (shhh!). When she's not designing covers, and writing or editing books, she's taking photos of them for her Instagram @colby_bettley. She also loves to talk to readers so don't hesitate to reach out and say hello!

You can find all her social media and relevant links at:

https://www.authorcolbybettley.com

www.ingramcontent.com/pod-product-compliance
Lightning Source LLC
Chambersburg PA
CBHW071437080526
44587CB00014B/1886